Music in the Liturgy

by
Ben Whitworth

All booklets are published thanks to the
generous support of the members of the
Catholic Truth Society

CATHOLIC TRUTH SOCIETY
PUBLISHERS TO THE HOLY SEE

Contents

All rights reserved. First published 2012 by The Incorporated Catholic Truth Society 40-46 Harleyford Road, London SE11 5AY Tel: 020 7640 0042 Fax: 020 7640 0046. Copyright © 2012 The Incorporated Catholic Truth Society.

ISBN 978 1 86082 811 9

Front cover: Singing Angels, Polyptych in St Bavo Cathedral, Ghent, Belgium by Jan Van Eyck. © Lukas - Art in Flanders VZW Photo: Hugo Maertens, www.bridgemanart.com.

Introduction:
Liturgical Music at the Crossroads?

The Christian community must make an examination of conscience so that the beauty of music and hymnody will return once again to the liturgy.[1]

(John Paul II)

Ignatius Kung was born in Shanghai in 1901. Ordained to the priesthood in 1930, he was appointed Bishop of Shanghai in 1950, just months after the Communists had come to power in China. As an implacable critic of the regime, he was arrested in 1955 and spent more than thirty years in prison. In 1985, he was allowed a visitor: Jaime Cardinal Sin of Manila. A formal dinner was arranged. The two cardinals (Pope John Paul II had secretly created Kung a cardinal six years before) were seated at opposite ends of a long banqueting table, with twenty Communist officials and collaborators between them. Conversation was, of course, impossible. Cardinal Sin had the inspiration of asking all the "guests" to sing their favourite song. When Cardinal Kung's turn came, he looked the Filipino prelate in the eyes and intoned a plainsong chant: *Tu es Petrus, et super hanc petram ædificabo ecclesiam meam.* "You are Peter, and on this rock I will build my Church". Ordered to be silent, the octogenarian cardinal continued the chant to the end, demonstrating to Cardinal Sin - and thus to the whole world - his continued loyalty to the Pope as the successor of St Peter.

An aged confessor of the faith passing a coded message is probably not the first image that comes to mind on hearing the phrase "music in the liturgy". But what Cardinal Kung chose to sing was a piece of liturgical music, and what made *Tu es Petrus* suitable for worship also made it suitable for the unconventional use to which he put it.

The chant uses a scriptural text (*Mt* 16:18): in this case, one which is often used in connection with the Catholic doctrine of the Papal primacy. It is part of the Gregorian chant repertoire which is foundational to Roman Catholic liturgical music. It is therefore part of an international musical "language"; a modern Chinese hymn, even one with the same theme, might not have communicated Kung's message quite so readily to the Filipino visitor. It is also sufficiently simple as a piece of music that it can be sung by a solo voice, even in such trying circumstances, and its musical form articulates the text rather than obscuring it. Finally, like all true liturgical music, *Tu es Petrus* is an act of praise. Cardinal Kung did not merely pass on a piece of information: he gave glory to God in his captivity. Scriptural, doctrinal, universal, articulate and prayerful: these qualities epitomise liturgical music.

A time of crisis

Sadly, in recent decades, liturgical music, which should unite us in sweet harmony, has become a subject of vehement debate within the Catholic Church. Pope Benedict XVI (writing when he was still Professor Ratzinger) did not hesitate to describe this as a "time of crisis" for church music;[2] his predecessor, Blessed John Paul II, even called the whole Church to "make an examination of conscience" on the subject of music in the liturgy. This booklet will give a brief account of the origins and development of Catholic liturgical music, of the role music plays within the liturgy, and of the theological theory which underpins the musical practice. It aims to be accurate and balanced, but not merely descriptive. It acknowledges that there is a crisis, and proposes a way forward from the crossroads that we have reached: the Church herself will provide our roadmap.

This booklet deals mainly with the kind of celebration at which readers are most likely to encounter music in the liturgy: Sunday Mass in the Ordinary Form of the Roman Rite (the Mass of Paul VI). In his *motu proprio* of 2007, *Summorum Pontificum*, Pope Benedict XVI made the Extraordinary Form of the Roman Mass (the traditional Latin Mass of Blessed Pope John XXIII) available to those who desire it. The Extraordinary Form has its own musical rules and customs, but many of the broad principles discussed in this booklet apply equally to this more ancient use; as the Holy Father has stated, "what earlier generations held as sacred, remains sacred and great for us too".[3]

Why Worshippers Sing

Singing is what a lover does.[4] (St Augustine)

All the major religions have their traditional ceremonial music. In Hindu temples, an ancient form of unison chanting known as *dhrupad* is performed to a percussion accompaniment. Sufi Islam has the *qawwali*, a genre of devotional song, highly formulaic but with an element of improvisation. Native American tribes have a tradition of sacred chant, as well as a kind of ritualised recitation, in which the rhythms and patterns of speech are formalised into a style that lies halfway between speaking and singing. The ancient Greeks, too, sang hymns in honour of their gods. Two of the hymns to Apollo even survive in a legible musical notation. Ritual and music are intimately connected.

Music in religious worship serves several purposes. The singing voice can often be clearer and more audible than the normal speaking voice. Aided by the acoustics of the liturgical space, the words of the Bible, when chanted, can be more easily heard and understood by a large congregation. A musical setting can also make the sacred texts of the liturgy more memorable, since most of us find it easier to learn a song by heart than a passage of prose.

The memorisation of commonly used texts makes it easier to take an active part in the rite; and it provides the believer with material on which to meditate outside of the service time. The early monks of the Egyptian desert, who chanted the Psalms as part of their daily prayer, often committed the whole Psalter to memory.

The emotive power of music

Just as secular songs can be a powerful vehicle for expressing our personal, natural emotions, so religious song can be expressive of the Church's "emotions": love of God, desire for communion with him, sorrow over sin. In as much as liturgical music is expressive, it enables us to address God. But *he* must also address *us* through the music we hear and sing in church. Liturgical music should stir in our hearts the love of God and neighbour. It should calm our passions and soothe our anxieties. It should instil contrition for our sins. Film-makers and advertisers understand the emotive power of music; the Church too is aware of this power, but uses it with restraint. Music that merely tugs at the heart-strings can degenerate into sentimentality. Above all, liturgical music should foster devotion: it should encourage that raising of the heart and mind to God which is the very essence of prayer.

Sacred song moves us as we hear or sing it, but its effect is not transitory. Liturgical music has a formative element; it changes people. Music performs this function whenever it makes a sacred text more noticeable, attractive and memorable; or when it interprets that text through the musical emphasis or repetition of important words. We can go further: music has a formative power in its own right. The ancient philosophers Plato and Aristotle held that music exercised an abiding moral influence on the listener.

Congregational singing

Congregational singing has a unitive function. If a large and miscellaneous group of people are to recite together a long text such as the *Gloria* or the Creed at Mass, then the use of a simple musical setting makes it easier to keep everyone in step. This is practically useful; but it also symbolises and engenders the unity of the faithful. In talking about unity between individuals we often use musical metaphors: "being in harmony", "singing from the same hymn sheet". These figures of speech are made concrete when Christians worship and sing together. Some people have even been tempted to exclude solo or choral music as being divisive: whatever is sung, they argue, must be sung by everyone. This overlooks the power that music possesses to bring its listeners, as well as its performers, into closer unity. Joseph Ratzinger has written about "the unity-creating power of shared listening, shared wonder".[5]

While the music of the liturgy binds the congregation together in the here and now, it can also forge and strengthen our bonds with the Church throughout the world, and throughout the ages. A music that is universal - or at the very least purged of any exclusively local traits - reminds us that we sing in communion with a worldwide Church. Today, when international gatherings are increasingly common, it is essential that all Catholics have access to a shared musical patrimony. Our sense of communion with other generations of believers is deepened whenever we sing or hear those works of liturgical music that have come down to us from the Christian past, and which we shall, please God, hand on to our own children.

Sacral styles

Certain musical styles and repertoires are fitter for those purposes than others. Music that is particularly suitable for liturgical use is traditionally, and rightly, called "sacred music". Like the fragrance of incense, such music will evoke holy rather than secular associations and sentiments in those who perform and hear it, offering us indeed a foretaste of heaven. Its sacral quality will - as far as is possible - be evident to all listeners, irrespective of their personal tastes or particular cultural background, and it will be easily distinguished from the commercial pop music which we hear all around us in today's noisy world. It will embody the highest artistic standards that can be achieved with the resources available: we must not give God what is second best. It will foster the unity of the people of God. It will draw on, and be congruent with, what the Second

Vatican Council called "a treasure of inestimable value":[6] the Church's bi-millennial musical tradition. If it is verbal music, orthodox texts will be used, and the words will not be obscured to the point of incomprehensibility.

Successive Popes and Councils have taken the view that the genre which best fulfils all these criteria is plainsong: the sacred chant that has co-evolved with the liturgy over the course of eighty generations. Other styles and repertoires which meet the criteria for sacred music also have a legitimate place in the liturgy.

Music in the Bible

They sing the song of Moses, the servant of God, and the song of the Lamb.

(Revelation 15:3)

Sacred scripture rings with the sound of music. As early as the fourth chapter of Genesis, we read about a son of Lamech, separated by only seven generations from Adam: "Jubal…was the ancestor of all who play the lyre and the flute" (*Gn* 4:21). Instrumental music, then, is seen by the inspired writer as being deeply rooted in the early origins of mankind. Archaeology tells a similar story: flutes made from bird bone and mammoth ivory, found in caves at Geissenklösterle (Germany), have been dated to between 42,000 and 43,000 years ago.

The first explicit reference to singing as an act of praise comes in the book of Exodus, in a passage which we hear each year during the Easter Vigil. Moses has led the Israelites safely out of Egypt, while Pharaoh's pursuing armies have been drowned. "It was then that Moses and the sons of Israel sang this song in honour of the Lord: 'The Lord I sing: he has covered himself in glory, horse and rider he has thrown into the sea'" (*Ex* 15:1). This response to the Israelites' miraculous escape appears to be spontaneous; but the whole of God's people participates in Moses' act of praise.

Temple music

Later, music was an element of the worship offered to God in the Temple at Jerusalem. When the Temple was solemnly dedicated, the Levitical singers accompanied themselves on cymbals, harps and lyres, and were joined by 120 priests with trumpets. "The trumpeters and singers [made] themselves heard in unison in praise and thanksgiving to the Lord, and when the song was raised...the glory of the Lord filled the house of God" (*2 Ch* 5:13-14 (RSV)). In this account, music of an extravagantly triumphant character appears to be the means of manifesting God's presence in his Temple. Thereafter, music was used in the Temple liturgies - to summon the faithful, and as what one early Christian writer called a "sacrifice of praise" (*Heb* 13:15) to accompany the sacrifices offered on the altar. Josephus, writing in the first century AD, confirms that the Levitical singers and musicians were still employed in the Temple in apostolic times.

The Psalter was the hymn book of the Temple; many of the Psalms are headed with instructions to the choirmaster. Music accompanied processions: "They see your solemn procession, O God, the procession of my God, of my King, to the sanctuary: the singers in the forefront, the musicians coming last, between them, maidens sounding their timbrels"

(*Ps* 67:25-26). Some Psalms (e.g. 66, 79, 135) have a repeated refrain, which may have been sung by the people as a whole.

Music in the New Testament

As a Jew, Jesus Christ was the inheritor of this long and rich tradition of music in worship. At the end of the Last Supper, immediately after the institution of the Eucharist, Christ and his apostles sang "psalms" before departing for the Mount of Olives (*Mt* 26:30; *Mk* 14:26). It is very likely that these "psalms" were *Hallel*. This is the recitation of Psalms 112 to 117, which Jews perform at the close of the Passover meal and on other religious feast days. Probably, the chanting of *Hallel* was something very familiar to the apostles - a ritual song that they would have known by heart.

This is the only explicit reference to religious music in the Gospels, but the other books of the New Testament demonstrate that the early Christians could not keep from singing, even when they were constrained to praise God in the most adverse circumstances. Saints Paul and Silas, imprisoned for sedition at Philippi, were "praying and singing hymns to God" at midnight when an earthquake struck and shattered their bonds (*Ac* 16:25 (RSV)). Luke notes that the other prisoners were listening to Paul and Silas; was the Apostle of the Gentiles using hymnody as a way of preaching? It is certainly the case that the evangelising power of music has been harnessed by later generations of Christians, from St Augustine of Canterbury to Billy Graham.

Paul urges Christians to sing together in praise of God. To the Church at Ephesus, he writes: "be filled with the Spirit, addressing one another in psalms and hymns and spiritual songs, singing and making melody to the Lord with all your heart" (*Ep* 5:18-19 (RSV)). He likewise counsels the Christians of Colossae, "Let the message of Christ, in all its richness, find a home with you... With gratitude in your hearts, sing psalms and hymns and inspired songs to God" (*Col* 3:16). Elsewhere, Paul demands that when the Christians of Corinth gather together, "let everyone be ready with a psalm or a sermon or a revelation, or ready to use his gift of tongues or to give an interpretation" (*1 Co* 14:26). The "Psalms" that Paul refers to are presumably those of the Old Testament. We cannot now be sure whether there is a significant distinction between "hymns" and "inspired songs", or whether Paul simply uses synonymous terms for rhetorical effect.

Early Christian hymns

Scholars have speculated that certain passages in the New Testament, written in a kind of rhythmic prose, are quotations from the earliest Christian hymns. For example, a fragment of song may be embedded in the letter to the Ephesians: "Wake up from your sleep, rise from the dead, and Christ will shine on you" (*Ep* 5:14). The use of song in early Christian worship is confirmed by a letter of Pliny the Younger to the Emperor Trajan (c. AD 111), in which he reports that the Christians "assemble at dawn on a fixed day, to sing a hymn antiphonally to Christ as God".[7]

In the book of Revelation, St John recounts a vision in which heaven is opened to him - and what is revealed is a heaven loud with song. John presents the reader with an ever-widening circle of sung praise. At first, it is only the four living creatures around the throne who sing. "Day and night they never stopped singing, 'Holy, Holy, Holy is the Lord God Almighty; he was, he is and he is to come!'" (*Rv* 4:8). Then we hear the chorus of the twenty-four elders (*Rv* 4:11), and the "new hymn" uttered by the living creatures and the elders together (*Rv* 5:9-10). Next, the 144,000 redeemed souls are described as singing a new song which none but they could learn (*Rv* 14:1-3); later, they sing "the hymn of Moses, the servant of God, and of the Lamb" beside a sea of glass (*Rv* 15:2-4). Their words echo the hymn that Moses sang on the shore of the Red Sea (*Ex* 15).

None of these passages gives us much detail about the practice or form of early Christian music, but these stray verses do at least allow us to deduce that the first followers of Christ sang the customary Jewish Psalms; and that they supplemented these with songs of specifically Christian content, addressing them to one another or directly to God; and that they looked forward to singing God's praises eternally in the hereafter.

Music and the Saints

There Magdalen hath left her moan,
And cheerfully doth sing
With blessed saints, whose harmony
In every street doth ring.
   (Anonymous, 'Jerusalem my happy home', c. 1600)

St Cecilia

If the Christian's hope is to spend eternity singing God's praises in heaven, it is small wonder that some of the best known saints are closely associated with music. The patron saint of musicians is St Cecilia, a Roman martyr of the third century. All we know about Cecilia comes from an unreliable fifth-century legend. This claims that she was a Roman lady of noble family who married the pagan Valerian. She succeeded in converting both him and his brother Tiburtius to Christianity. The two brothers were martyred for the faith, and Cecilia arranged their burial. This work of mercy towards her dead menfolk brought Cecilia to the attention of the authorities. She was condemned to be suffocated, but survived the ordeal; a soldier was ordered to decapitate her, but three blows failed to kill her, and she died of her wounds some days later. Her body was interred in the Catacombs of

St Callistus, and her house in Trastevere was consecrated as a church by the Pope of the time, St Urban I.

At morning and evening prayer on her feast day (22nd November), the Liturgy of the Hours quotes a passage from her legend, describing how Cecilia was unmoved by the music at her wedding banquet: "While the organs were making melody, Cecilia sang to the Lord over and over: 'Let my heart be pure, and let me not be put to shame'." In the legend, a contrast is drawn between the sensual organ music and Cecilia's chaste utterance. Taken out of context, however, the sentence makes it sound as though the Saint was actually singing to the accompaniment of organs. Owing perhaps to a misunderstanding of this kind, the tradition arose by the fourteenth century of depicting St Cecilia with an organ. Music festivals were held on her feast day in France from 1570, and later in England. Many famous choral works were composed for these occasions, notably the *Odes to St Cecilia* by Henry Purcell, and by GF Handel.

St Gregory the Great

There is one other saint who sometimes challenges Cecilia for the title of patron of musicians, or at least of church singers. Pope St Gregory I (d. 604), justly titled "the Great", has traditionally been credited with the codification, or even the composition, of the Roman chant repertoire. In fact, Gregory's sole known pronouncement on sacred music is less than enthusiastic. It seems that during Gregory's papacy most of the singing at Mass was being done by deacons. This troubled Gregory on two counts: because the singing of psalms was a distraction from the deacon's other duties; and because the admiration shown towards fine singers could give rise to a vanity that would be unbecoming in an ordained clergyman. Gregory ruled that singers were to be drawn from the lower orders of the clergy: subdeacons, acolytes, lectors and so on. While Gregory does not doubt that singing in church is legitimate and valuable, he appears here as a regulator, not a propagator, of liturgical music.

Why then do chant books from the eighth century onwards refer to Pope Gregory as the compiler of the Mass Proper - the special chants for each Sunday and feast day? One possible answer is that the earliest manuscripts were actually referring to Pope St Gregory II (d. 731), whose papacy coincided with the completion of the Proper. Be that as it may, the presumed connection between the first Gregory, and the music that we now call "Gregorian chant", has been firmly fixed in the Christian consciousness for many centuries.

SS Ephrem, Ambrose and Benedict

There are other saints who were themselves music makers. St Ephrem of Syria (d. 373), known as the Harp of the Holy Spirit, was a monk, scholar and hymn writer. His hymns helped to reinforce the orthodoxy, and sustain the morale, of Christians besieged in Edessa by an army of Arian heretics. In similar circumstances, St Ambrose, Bishop of Milan (d. 397), introduced congregational hymn singing to the Western Church. At a time of persecution by an Arian Emperor, Ambrose and his people found themselves besieged in a suburban church. To raise the people's spirits during the blockade, Ambrose taught them to sing hymns of his own composition. St Benedict of Nursia (d. c. 550) drew up a Rule for monks which was to become the standard guide to monastic life in the West. Benedict took great care to arrange the Psalms and hymns that would be sung during the seven daily offices of prayer. He also gave his monks the following advice on *how* the Divine Office should be sung:

> Let us ever remember the words of the prophet: "Serve ye the Lord in fear" (*Ps* 2:11); and again, "Sing ye wisely" (*Ps* 46:8); and, "In the sight of the angels will I sing to thee" (*Ps* 137:2). Let us then consider how we ought to behave ourselves in the presence of God and his angels, and so sing the Psalms that mind and voice may be in harmony.[8]

St Philip Neri

One saint who played a significant role in the development of sacred music was St Philip Neri (1515-1595). In the 1530s and 1540s, Philip spent his time working among the poor, the sick and the young people of Rome, while living a life of strict asceticism. He devoted his afternoons to boys and young men, encouraging them in works of piety and practical charity, and instructed them at his lodgings. Philip was ordained a priest in 1551, and was assigned to the church of San Girolamo. There he built a gallery above the church, and instead of meeting in his rooms, men of every class now gathered in this "oratory" to pray together. As well as sermons, readings, prayers and meditations, these services included music. The director of music for the oratory was the great composer Giovanni Pierluigi da Palestrina (c. 1525-1594), so it goes without saying that the artistic standards of this music were extremely high. In 1583, Philip moved his oratory exercises to a new church (still called the Chiesa Nuova), which was staffed by a community of the saint's priest-disciples. This community was called the Congregation of the Oratory, since the oratory services were such a central part of their apostolate. The term *oratorio* was also applied to the services themselves, and, by extension, to other performances of religious music outside of a strictly liturgical context: hence the "oratorios" of Bach, Handel and Mendelssohn. On 25th May 1595, which was the feast of Corpus Christi, St Philip celebrated Low Mass as usual, but he sang the whole of the *Gloria in excelsis* with great joy and devotion. That night, he went to God.

The Congregation of the Oratory was introduced into England by Blessed John Henry Newman. Newman himself was an accomplished violinist, who used to entertain his confrères with his performances, especially of Beethoven's music. As a young man, he even composed music with some skill, writing under the name Neandrini - a jocular Italianisation of "Newman". The Oratory churches of London, Birmingham and Oxford continue to offer musical oratories in the tradition of St Philip. Newman's own foundation, the Birmingham Oratory, is also now the home of the Blessed John Henry Newman Institute of Liturgical Music, which offers training in sacred music for clergy, singers and organists.

Towards a Theology of Music

It seems that relations between theology and church music have always been somewhat cool.[9]

(Joseph Ratzinger)

The Greek philosophers

Despite the importance of music in the liturgy, serious and sustained discourse about music has been rare in the Christian theological tradition. Often, Christian thinkers have taken their cues from the Greek philosophers Pythagoras, Plato and Aristotle. Pythagoras (d. c. 475 BC) discovered the connections between mathematics and music, and he held that the movement of the celestial bodies was governed by mathematical patterns that generated a kind of inaudible music: the harmony of the spheres. This harmony was replicated in the human body and soul, and imitated in the music that we play. The notion that men, and the heavens, are in some sense inherently musical, proved a fruitful idea for Christian thinkers, even if they did not accept all of Pythagoras's theories about the universe and humanity.

Plato (d. 347 BC) endorsed the Pythagorean analogy between music and the human person. Plato attributed a formative power to music: its harmonies could restore us to inner harmony, and make us better, healthier people. In the *Timaeus*, he contrasts this ethical view of music with the vulgar idea that music is merely pleasurable:

> All audible musical sound is given us by the gods for the sake of harmony, which has motions akin to the orbits in our soul, and which, as anyone who makes intelligent use of the arts knows, is not to be used, as is commonly thought, to give irrational pleasure, but as a heaven-sent ally in reducing to order and harmony any disharmony in the revolutions within us.[10]

In the *Laws*, Plato complained that the poets who wrote for the stage in his day had lost the ability to judge music: "In their mindlessness they involuntarily falsified music itself when they asserted that there was no such thing as correct music, and that it was quite correct to judge music by the standard of the pleasure it gives to whoever enjoys it."[11] The result was an inversion of proper values: by indulging their weaknesses, bad music shaped people's characters for ill.

According to the *Politics* of Aristotle (d. 322 BC), music may legitimately be enjoyed in a purely recreational way. Nevertheless, Aristotle still subordinates the sensual and intellectual pleasures of music to its character-forming properties, and warns against valuing its recreational benefits more highly than its ethical ones. Aristotle recommends the teaching of music to the young, on account of its power to form the character; but he cautions against teaching them certain instruments, such as the flute and the lyre, which lend themselves to showy virtuosity.

The Church Fathers

Some of the earliest ecclesiastical writers share something of Pythagoras's optimism about music. St Clement of Rome, writing around AD 95, draws a parallel between the song of the angels around the throne of God, and the song of the Christian people gathered for the Eucharist. The parallel is all the more striking because the words attributed to the angels in Isaiah already formed part of the Christian liturgy. Thus Clement writes:

> Think of the vast company of his angels, who all wait on him to serve his wishes. "Ten thousand times ten thousand stood before him," says Scripture, "and thousand thousands did him service (*Dn* 7:10), crying, 'Holy, holy, holy is the Lord of hosts; all creation is full of his glory' (*Is* 6:3)." In the same way ought we ourselves, gathered together in a conscious unity, to cry to him as it were with a single voice, if we are to obtain a share of his glorious great promises.[12]

The idea that liturgical singing is a participation in the song of the angels was to become a common motif in Christian writing.

St Ignatius of Antioch, writing to the Church at Ephesus in the first quarter of the second century, makes an extensive analogy between the social harmony existing among the members of the church, and the blending of their voices in musical praise:

> Your justly respected clergy, who are a credit to God, are attuned to their bishop like the strings of a harp, and the result is a hymn of praise to Jesus Christ from minds that are in unison, and affections that are in harmony. Pray, then, come and join this choir, every one of you; let there be a whole symphony of minds in concert; take the tone all together from God, and sing aloud to the Father with one voice through Jesus Christ, so that he may hear you and know by your good works that you are indeed members of his Son's Body.[13]

On the other hand, some of the Fathers of the Church echoed Plato's reservations about the misuse of music. St Jerome (d. 419), was caustic in his criticism of vain young men who belted out theatrical melodies in church. He certainly did not wish to abolish liturgical music, but insisted that musicians should exercise their ministry by singing to God with their hearts - not just playing to the gallery with their voices.

St Augustine

Jerome's younger contemporary, St Augustine (d. 430), took a similarly ambivalent view of church music. In his candid autobiography, the *Confessions*, Augustine explains his dilemma. At times, he regrets that he has given more honour to the singer's performance than to the words; in this mood, he wishes "that every note of the delightful tunes to which the Psalms of David are commonly sung, should be banished from my ears, and indeed from the Church's hearing".[14] At other times, he thanks God for the music that heightened his appreciation of divine truth: "Hearing your hymns and canticles, how I wept, deeply moved by the sweet-sounding voices of your Church! Those voices poured into my ears, and truth flowed into my heart, and thence feelings of piety bubbled over, and tears ran, and I was all the better for them."[15] The saying, "He who sings, prays twice," is often attributed to Augustine; while these words are not actually found in his writings, they do perfectly encapsulate the more positive side of his attitude towards music. Augustine concluded that church music is beneficial, but his approval was qualified. He suggested that music is added to words because it rouses the devotion of "weaker souls" - the words themselves ought to be enough for the devout. Furthermore, the chanting of Psalms should be "closer to speaking than to singing";[16] and the listener must be on guard, under pain of sin, against taking an excessive pleasure in the music itself.

St Hildegard of Bingen

A more unequivocally positive theology of music was formulated by a woman who was herself one of the earliest named composers of sacred music. St Hildegard of Bingen

(1098-1179) was a Benedictine nun and visionary from the Rhineland who became abbess of her nunnery at the age of thirty-eight. She composed seventy-seven monodic chants for female voices, as well as an allegorical music drama, the *Play of the Virtues*. These were all presumably intended for use by her nuns at St Rupertsberg. Hildegard told Volmar, her secretary and biographer, that her compositions were not the result of any musical learning or craft, but were simply revealed to her by God.

Hildegard's thinking about music reflects the Pythagorean ideas of cosmic and anthropic harmony. In the *Play of the Virtues*, the only character who does not sing his lines is the devil: he shouts. As Hildegard explained, Satan was troubled by the sweet singing of Adam in the garden, since it reminded him of the lost harmonies of heaven. The evil one has ever since made it his business "to disturb or destroy the affirmation and beauty and sweetness of divine praise and spiritual hymns".[17] Song is related not only to the music of the spheres and the harmony of the soul, but to the praises offered by the angels in heaven. In her sequence for St Rupert (*O Jerusalem*), Hildegard addresses the patron saint of her nunnery: "In you the Holy Spirit makes symphony (*symphonizat*), for you are joined with the angelic choirs." Indeed, in the Incarnation, the music of heaven is heard upon the earth. In a hymn to the Virgin (*Ave generosa*), Hildegard writes: "There was joy in your womb when all the celestial symphony sounded forth from you, for you, a virgin, bore the Son of God". Vocal music has a special value for Hildegard, since it uses a natural instrument - one created by God rather than fashioned by human craftsmen.

Towards the end of Hildegard's life, a dispute arose between the St Rupertsburg nuns and the canons of Mainz Cathedral. The canons punished the nuns for an alleged act of disobedience by ruling that they should only speak the words of the Divine Office instead of singing them. To Hildegard, this was a torment. The Archbishop of Mainz eventually overruled this petty interdict, but not before Hildegard had written one of her most eloquent letters in protest. She declared that Adam, in Eden, sang with the angels so that his voice became like that of an angel; in his voice could be heard all harmony and all musical art. "Had he remained in the state in which he was created, the weaknesses of human mortality could never have robbed that voice of its strength and sonority."[18] Only in our own singing can we hope to recapture the sweetness of that song of Eden. Pope Benedict has recently extended the cult of St Hildegard to the universal Church, and on 7th October 2012 he will formally proclaim her a Doctor of the Church. It is to be hoped that these moves will attract renewed attention to Hildegard's writings on music.

St Thomas Aquinas

St Thomas Aquinas (d. 1274) was educated by Benedictine monks, and the chanting of the Divine Office was his lifelong delight. He wrote that the Psalter contains within itself the entire substance of theology, and he was frequently moved to tears while singing the Psalms. In his theological work, he quoted ancient hymns as evidence of the Church's doctrines, and he wrote the words to some of the best known hymns of Eucharistic devotion: *Pange lingua*, *Adoro te* and *Lauda Sion*.

When Aquinas touched on the subject of liturgical music in his *Summa Theologica*, he made three principal points: that music is beneficial because it arouses devotion; that it should not be accompanied by instruments that serve only to give pleasure to the senses; and that one who sings in a devotional spirit does not obscure the meaning of the words, but articulates them all the more clearly. Aquinas's objection to *some* instruments - he specifies the harp and the psaltery (a harp with a soundbox) - does not imply an outright rejection of instrumental accompaniment in the liturgy. We need to bear in mind that the pipe organ was already in general use as a liturgical instrument by the time Aquinas was writing; but like Aristotle, whom he cites, Aquinas simply felt that some instruments were better suited to serious music than others. Similarly, although he insists that liturgical music is addressed to the mind, and not simply to the ear, Aquinas does not think it necessary that every word should be audible or instantly comprehensible: "Even if those who listen sometimes do not understand the words being sung, they do understand the reason for the singing, namely, the praise of God. And that is sufficient to arouse men to worship."[19]

Prof. Joseph Ratzinger

The Catholic theological tradition, then, leaves us with some powerful but disconnected statements about music, many of them reliant on the pre-Christian thinking of the Greek philosophers. If we have, in recent decades, advanced some way towards a fuller and more coherent theology of music, it is largely thanks to the present Pope. Benedict XVI's love of music is well known, and he is said to relax by playing the music of Mozart on the piano. As a Professor of Theology, as a Vatican Cardinal, and indeed as Pope, Joseph Ratzinger has returned many times to the theological questions concerning music in general, and especially music in the liturgy.

In a 1974 essay (published in English in *The Feast of Faith*), Ratzinger examines the theological basis of church music. He acknowledges that "relations between theology and church music have always been somewhat cool",[20] and blames this on the lingering legacy of Plato and Aristotle. The Christian has other sources from which to draw a positive theology of religious music. Ratzinger makes an analogy with the veneration of icons, in which the senses are not treated as obstacles to a "pure" spiritual religion, but are made the very means of prayer and worship. He points to the Psalms, inherited from the Temple and integral to the worship of the Church: these show no reticence in exhorting us to praise God with vocal and instrumental music. The Psalms also teach us to integrate our song with the wordless praise offered by the whole of creation: "The heavens proclaim the glory of God" (*Ps* 18:1). The deep delight we experience when we participate in sung liturgy is itself an argument for the goodness of liturgical song. Both Augustine and Aquinas fluctuate between their deep emotional response to the beauty of church music, and the somewhat puritanical strictures that they derive from classical philosophy. For Ratzinger, the beauty itself is good for the soul.

Ratzinger took up these themes again in his later writings, and returned to them at length in a chapter of *The Spirit of the Liturgy* (2000). Here he explores in greater depth the ways in which liturgical music is connected with the word (*logos*). The primacy, in music for the liturgy, is always given to the singing of *words* - of the liturgical text, which is generally scriptural in origin - though without excluding instrumental music. At a deeper level, liturgical song is associated with *the* Word: Jesus Christ. The measure of music's suitability for liturgical worship is the extent to which it draws the soul upwards, under the impulsion of the Holy Spirit, towards God in Christ. In another sense again, the word *logos* is used by Greek philosophers and the New Testament writers alike to designate human reason, and the divine rationality underlying the cosmic order. In a way that Pythagoras would have recognised, Christian music seeks to harmonise itself with the *logos* in this sense. Liturgical music places us in a cosmic chorus of praise that joins our voices with those of the angels and saints around the throne of the Lamb. Music and Word are no longer in opposition - as they were, at times, in the writings of Jerome, Augustine and Aquinas - but blended together in the "new song" that is Christian worship.

The Tradition

*Here we have a musical tradition which has sprung
from the very heart of the Church and her faith.*[21]

(Joseph Ratzinger)

As with many other aspects of worship, for the origins
of Christian music we must look to the Jewish milieu in
which the infant Church grew up. There was - as we have
seen from the Old Testament evidence - a tradition of using
music in the worship of the Temple. In the Synagogue
too, singing formed an integral part of the service, though
here it was unaccompanied. Unfortunately, we do not
have notated music from this period of Jewish history, but
later evidence may give us some clues as to what *might*
have been sung in the time of Christ. As early as the sixth
century, the Jewish scholars (*masoretes*) who copied the
text of the Hebrew Bible began to introduce a rudimentary
notation, indicating where a reader in the Synagogue was
to raise or lower the pitch of his voice. These Masoretic
signs may well be the first written record of a performance
technique that had previously been transmitted through the
oral tradition. What they indicate is a style of performance
known as "cantillation" - somewhere between reading and
singing, which does no more than formalise or heighten

the patterns inherent in speech itself. This form of chanting can help the sound to carry, and it irons out the peculiarities of the individual's voice and diction. When we hear of Jesus reading from the scroll of Isaiah in the Synagogue (*Lk* 4:16-20), we could imagine him chanting the prophet's words in this manner.

Since the first Christians continued to worship in the Synagogue until their expulsion in around AD 80, it is reasonable to surmise that early Christian music may have taken its inspiration and its form from Jewish cantillation. Indeed, there are striking similarities between some Gregorian chants and some of the Masoretic cantillations, though we cannot with certainty trace these parallels further back than the late first millennium.

Church singers

By the middle of the fourth century, the church singer (called the *psaltes*) had a distinct ministry within the liturgy. The Council of Laodicea (364) decreed that no one should ascend the pulpit to sing the Psalms except a competent *psaltes* who had been canonically appointed to his office. This does not mean that the congregation remained dumb, since there is evidence that the people sang responses to the Psalms. Some time between the fourth and seventh centuries, there was a further development in church music at Rome: this was the creation of the *schola cantorum*, the choir of trained musicians who sang at the Pope's Mass. The emergence of this musical elite allowed a more complex style of chant to develop alongside the simple solo and responsorial repertoire that already existed. By the early eighth century, the Papal *schola* had created a repertoire of nearly six hundred chants proper to the different feasts and seasons of the Church's year. This repertoire is still at the core of the *Graduale Romanum*, the choir book which contains the music for Mass in the Roman Rite.

Meanwhile, the tradition of unaccompanied, monodic chant was developing in slightly different directions at the various centres of the Christian world. These chants were often sung in a sacral form of the local language, such as Greek, Syriac, or Coptic. By the time that the *schola cantorum* was established, the liturgical language of the West was uniformly Latin. We have evidence for five different "families" of early Latin chant:

- Roman chant (which, for reasons that will become clear, is usually now referred to as *Old* Roman chant);

- Ambrosian chant at Milan;

- Beneventan chant at the southern Italian centres of Benevento and Montecassino;

- Mozarabic chant in Spain, Portugal and Pyrenean France;

- Gallican chant in France and (possibly) Ireland.

Gregorian chant

Gregorian chant arose from the marriage between the Old Roman and Gallican traditions. In the time of the Emperors Pepin, Charlemagne, and Louis the Pious, who ruled over much of what is now France and Germany in the eighth and ninth centuries, there were frequent exchanges of choir books and personnel between the Papal *schola* and the important churches in the Imperial territories. The Gallican choirs adopted the texts and basic melodies that were brought to them by the Papal cantors; but they interpreted them according to their own more expressive tradition, with shorter melodic formulae, but wider ranges of pitch and more abrupt intervals. The resulting fusion, which we call Gregorian chant, spread through most of the Latin Church in the course of the ninth and tenth centuries. At Rome itself, the Old Roman tradition persisted for a long time, but it was gradually supplanted by the Gregorian style between the eleventh and thirteenth centuries.

Organum

Up until this point, I have been describing the development of plainsong: vocal music sung on a single melodic line, without harmony or counterpoint. The introduction of a second voice, singing above or below the principal melodic line, represents another watershed in the development of liturgical music. This was probably an innovation of the ninth century, and the first large collection of music written in this style (known as "*organum*") is a tenth-century English manuscript, the Winchester Troper. In typical *organum*, one singer (the "tenor") sang the Gregorian melody, while a second singer - chanting the same text, and matching the rhythm of the tenor - sang at an interval of a fourth or fifth.

In the major centres of medieval culture, this basic *organum* was the seedbed for a profusion of new musical styles and techniques. At Notre Dame Cathedral in Paris, for example, the twelfth century saw the development of a much more elaborate *organum*. In the works of Leonin and Perotin, the low-voiced tenor stretches out the notes of the Gregorian melody to enormous, drone-like length, while as many as three higher voices sing convoluted lines above it. In this development, the sense of the words is practically lost to the listener, and the florid style was decried as effeminate by some critics at the time. Nevertheless, the "Notre Dame School" of *organum* was widely influential: one of the key manuscripts containing this music was used at St Andrews in Scotland, and it is thought to contain Scottish compositions alongside those of Leonin and Perotin. Besides settings of the actual liturgical texts, composers of this period also began to write motets: choral arrangements of religious texts which could be sung as extra musical adornments to the liturgy.

A further stylistic shift occurred in the early fifteenth century, with an English composer leading the way. The work of John Dunstable (or Dunstaple) from St Albans, drew on earlier forms of *organum*, but it used new intervals - the third and the sixth - to create a sweeter sound. His work is no easier for the listener, however, especially in those pieces where the different voices sing two or more different texts simultaneously! Dunstable's music was sung throughout Western Europe, and his enriched harmonic palette was influential on the development of polyphony in the sixteenth century.

Polyphony

That century would come to be marked by the emergence of the intellectual movement known as Humanism. The first Humanists (men like Erasmus of Rotterdam, the friend of St Thomas More) were preoccupied with textual purity, and they pioneered scholarly methods that helped to produce more accurate versions both of classical literary works and of the Bible itself. This renewed attention to words prompted a reaction against the extravagances of some musical settings. One Robert Richardson, a Scottish monk, typified the Humanist critique of contemporary church music. Writing in 1530, he held up Gregorian chant as the ideal, since it did not obscure the words of the liturgical texts. The simpler forms of polyphony were also acceptable, however: "that music is also worthy of commendation, in which the meaning can be taken in along with the melody...such song is pleasing to God and to men, and its singers and composers have merit".[22]

By the time that church music came up for discussion at the Council of Trent in 1562 and 1563, the Renaissance polyphonic style of singing was in its ascendancy. In this style, there is no longer a single dominant voice. Instead, the different parts are more or less equal, and several melodic lines are woven together to create a seamless garment of sound. Most cathedrals and other major churches had boys' choirs by this time, often fed by an affiliated "song school". This allowed composers to use a much wider range of voices, from treble to bass, further enriching the expressive possibilities of polyphony. Leading churchmen of the time - including Pope Marcellus II (reigned 1555) and St Charles Borromeo (1538-1584), the reforming Archbishop of Milan - shared the Humanists' anxieties: some settings were so elaborate that the words of the liturgy could not be heard or understood.

Renaissance polyphony

There is an old legend that the bishops assembled at the Council of Trent voted to ban polyphony altogether, but changed their mind after hearing Palestrina's *Missa Papae Marcelli*. It probably did not happen quite like that, but what is certain is that a commission of cardinals was convened in 1565 - two years after the Council ended - to hear specimens of polyphonic Mass settings sung by the Sistine Chapel Choir; and certainly, Palestrina was one of the composers whose work best reflects the

Humanists' concern for intelligibility. In fact, Palestrina's reputation was so high for centuries that he - and he alone - was sometimes named in Papal pronouncements as the composer whose music should be imitated in liturgical compositions.

Palestrina's music deserves still to be heard in the liturgical setting for which it was written; but Renaissance polyphony was an international style, and other liturgical composers from the same period have just as much to offer. Outstanding examples of the style include the Requiem Mass, and the Tenebrae Responsories for Holy Week, by Tomás Luis de Victoria (1548-1611), a Spanish Oratorian priest; the Requiem of Orlande de Lassus (1532-1594) from Flanders; and the Latin polyphony of two Catholic composers who lived and worked through the English Reformation, Thomas Tallis (c. 1505-1585) and William Byrd (1543-1623). Byrd's Masses for three, four and five voices were written to be sung in recusant chapels during the Elizabethan persecution.

Baroque music

The changes in church music during the seventeenth and eighteenth centuries reflect broader currents in the musical culture. The prestige of sacred music was somewhat eclipsed by the rising status of the opera and the orchestral symphony. The greatest employer of singers was no longer the Church but the opera house, and singers who performed on stage during the week inevitably brought a certain theatrical style and swagger into the church on Sunday. Now we begin to hear Baroque compositions that treat the sacred texts as drama. In works like the Vespers of the Blessed Virgin Mary (1610), written for St Mark's Cathedral, Venice by Claudio Monteverdi (1567-1643), or the famous *Gloria* of Antonio Vivaldi (1678-1741), the liturgical Latin is interpreted in a medley of galloping choruses, solo arias and instrumental sonatas. These masterpieces remain favourites in the concert hall. Less dazzling, but better suited to liturgical use, are works by composers like Henri Dumont (1610-1684), whose music stays closer to the spirit of chant and classic polyphony.

By the time of WA Mozart (1756-1791) and Joseph Haydn (1732-1809), Mass settings were effectively choral symphonies, with orchestral accompaniment and instrumental interludes. The constituent parts of the Mass Ordinary (*Kyrie, Gloria, Credo, Sanctus, Agnus Dei*) were broken up into "movements", with an alternation between solo arias and choruses. At its worst, the orchestral Mass or "concerted Mass" was indeed more like a concert than an act of divine worship. The musicians simply got on with their virtuoso performance, while the clergy got on with the celebration of Mass in the sanctuary, and neither party paid attention to what the other was doing. No one doubts the quality of the music, but it could be fairly said that the artistic tail was wagging the liturgical dog.

Even at the time, objections were raised to the worst extravagances of these concerted Masses. Under the influence of Enlightenment thought, the Emperor Joseph II of Austria urged composers to write shorter, more sober Mass settings in which the words could be clearly heard. The Emperor's views were echoed by church leaders like Archbishop Colloredo of Salzburg, who was at one time Mozart's employer. These principles were brought to bear on works such as Mozart's "Coronation" Mass in C Major (K.317), which dispatches the Mass Ordinary in less than half an hour - not much longer than some Gregorian Masses. The more suitable orchestral settings of the Mass may still be used liturgically: on Pentecost Sunday 2009, the 200th anniversary of Haydn's death, his *Harmoniemesse* was performed at the Papal Mass in St Peter's. The classical composers should not be placed in opposition to traditional sacred music: Mozart himself said that he would have given all of his own compositions to have written the plainsong Preface of the Mass.

The decline of chant

And what of the chant? How did the Church's ancient plainsong fare during these centuries of musical innovation? Sadly, chant was experiencing a long decline. The basic obstacle to the widespread use of Gregorian chant has always been the difficulty of singing the Proper of the Mass. This difficulty comes not from any inherent complexity in the music itself, which consists of monodic chants covering a modest range of pitches and lasting only a few minutes each. The problem comes from the fact that the Proper - as composed for the Papal *schola* in the seventh and eighth centuries, and added to during the middle ages - demands a completely different set of chants for every Sunday in the year, for every major feast, and even for every day during Lent. This means that a community can use the full Proper only if it possesses a group of competent singers who have the leisure to rehearse intensively every week. For the Papal chapel, a monastery or a cathedral, this is not a problem, but for parishes it can be a struggle.

The first, and worst, solution to this problem is simply to omit the singing of the Proper. With the development of Low Mass in the middle ages, it became customary for the priest alone to recite the text of the Proper in a speaking voice or monotone at the altar. Later, it was considered sufficient for the priest to recite the Proper in this way even at sung Masses; this left the choir free to concentrate on their ever more elaborate settings of the Mass Ordinary. The second expedient was to simplify the Proper chants. Palestrina began this process, but it was completed by less able hands, and the so-called Medicean Editions of the seventeenth century contained brutal truncations of the ancient melodies.

Restoration

The restoration of Gregorian chant began in earnest at the Benedictine monastery of Solesmes (France), which was founded in 1833 by Abbot Prosper Guéranger. He found liturgical chant in its decadence, undervalued and misunderstood, and he commissioned his monks to bring the Church's plainsong back to its pristine state. This was done, over the course of generations, by the painstaking collation and interpretation of the earliest manuscripts. Throughout the twentieth century, the Church lent her authority to the chant books produced at Solesmes, such as the *Graduale Romanum* ("Roman Gradual") which contains the chants for the Mass. Chant scholarship moves on, and there are now rival editions which reconstruct the music according to different methodologies, but the Solesmes books continue to be very widely used.

Pope St Pius X put chant at the centre of his renewed effort to purify church music in the early years of the twentieth century. The Pope's instruction on sacred music, *Tra le sollecitudini* (1903), contained a number of regulations aimed at eliminating the operatic style of music at Mass. *Tra le sollecitudini* recommended Palestrina as a model of liturgical composition, promoted the use of Gregorian chant, and encouraged the people to sing the parts of the Mass that belonged to them. At the level of general principle, St Pius X stated that sacred music should have the following characteristics: holiness, beauty (in Italian: *la bontà delle forme*), and universality. This triad of fundamental values has been repeated in subsequent Papal teaching on music.

The early twentieth century witnessed a widespread rediscovery of chant and Renaissance polyphony. It is said that when the London Oratory choir sang a Palestrina Mass on Easter Sunday for the first time, in place of the usual Mozart, people walked out in disgust, but the tide had turned. Modern church composers such as Gabriel Fauré (1845-1924), Maurice Duruflé (1902-1986) and Olivier Messiaen (1908-1992) turned to Gregorian chant for their inspiration. The movement to revive sacred music was not concerned only with compositions for choirs: much effort went into encouraging the laity to participate at sung Masses. This was no elitist pursuit; one of the keenest promoters of Gregorian chant in parishes was Dorothy Day, the founder of the Catholic Worker movement.

The Second Vatican Council and Beyond

The treasure of sacred music is to be preserved and fostered with great care.

(*Sacrosanctum Concilium* 114)

The first document promulgated by the Second Vatican Council was the Constitution on the Sacred Liturgy: *Sacrosanctum Concilium*. Its sixth chapter, devoted to "Sacred Music", is very much in line with the principles of St Pius X. *Sacrosanctum Concilium* teaches that "the musical tradition of the universal Church is a treasure of inestimable value, greater even than that of any other art. The main reason for this pre-eminence is that, as sacred song united to the words, it forms a necessary or integral part of the solemn liturgy" (SC 112).

The Council goes on to state that "Gregorian chant is specially suited to the Roman liturgy", and that "it should be given first place in liturgical services" (SC 116). Other forms of music - polyphony is mentioned - are "by no means excluded from liturgical celebrations" as long as "they accord with the spirit of the liturgical action" (SC 116), and "choirs must be diligently promoted" (SC 114). The Council fathers wax lyrical in praise of the pipe organ: "it adds a wonderful splendour to the Church's ceremonies and powerfully lifts up man's mind to God and to higher things" (SC 120).

Vernacular Mass settings

The Council itself was adamant that vernacular Mass settings should not entirely replace the traditional people's chants: "Steps should be taken so that the faithful may also be able to say or to sing together in Latin those parts of the Ordinary of the Mass which pertain to them" (SC 54). Pope Paul VI took such steps in 1974, when he ordered the publication of a booklet called *Jubilate Deo*. This contained what was described as a "minimum repertoire" of Gregorian chant: music for the Mass and for Benediction, with assorted chants in honour of our Lady and for other occasions. The introduction explains the booklet's purpose: "The Supreme Pontiff Paul VI wants the voices of the faithful to ring out in Gregorian chant as well as in vernacular hymns and songs".[23]

Simplified chants

Another measure that was ordered by the Council itself, was the compilation of a simplified book of chants for the use of small churches. The *Graduale Simplex* ("Simple Gradual") was put together by the monks of Solesmes and published by the Vatican in 1967, with a new edition in 1975. It includes some of the less complicated people's chants from the *Graduale Romanum*, but it replaces the variable weekly Proper with sets of seasonal chants in responsorial form. The *Simplex* was an ingenious piece of work, but it has never been widely used. Instead, what tended to happen in parishes is that vernacular hymns were introduced, effectively driving out any form of chanted Propers. The question of hymn-singing at Mass is a complex one, which will be dealt with in another chapter.

Now that congregations had Mass settings in their own language, and could sing hymns as substitutes for the Proper, what role was left for the choir? Very little, it must have seemed; and in spite of the Council's earnest plea to promote choral singing, the post-Conciliar period saw the near extinction of Catholic parish choirs.

New instruments

Similarly, the rise of guitar-led folk groups tended to eclipse the traditional status of the organ; this was never the will of the Church. The pipe organ has had a distinguished record of liturgical service. It was used in some English churches as early as the tenth century. In the later middle ages, chanting would be accompanied on the harp in some Northern countries, and from around 1600, the orchestra was deployed in Mass settings, but the organ has remained the pre-eminent instrument of church music. At first, the instrument merely accompanied a melodic line, or added an extra, wordless "voice" to some of the early forms of polyphony, but it has been heard as a solo instrument at

Mass since the Baroque period. When blessing a new organ at Regensburg in 2006, Pope Benedict eulogised the instrument: "The organ has always been considered, and rightly so, the king of musical instruments, because it takes up all the sounds of creation, and gives resonance to the fullness of human sentiments, from joy to sadness, from praise to lamentation".[24] The organ is perfectly suited to its role: it can fill the church with jubilant sound, or whisper in gentle reflection; as its note can be sustained, it is better for supporting singing voices than instruments whose notes quickly die away (such as the piano); and its sound is almost exclusively associated with Christian worship.

The Council decreed that other instruments may be permitted by the local bishops' conference, provided that they are suitable for sacred use, that they "accord with the dignity of the temple" (SC 120), and that they truly edify the faithful. The instruments of the classical orchestra, already hallowed by centuries of liturgical use, surely have rights of domicile in the church. Whether the use of instruments primarily associated with secular pop music can be reconciled with the Council's criteria, is a question that bishops' conferences must settle with the utmost discretion. The rejection of strummed string instruments by Aristotle and Aquinas need not determine the issue, but it shows that the question is far from new.

If pastoral practice has tended to drift away from the guidelines laid down by *Sacrosanctum Concilium* over the last fifty years, there is evidence that Catholics in many places are returning to forms of liturgical music more in keeping with what the Council proposed. Gregorian chant has survived as liturgical music - not merely as an art form - thanks largely to a few monasteries, and to inspired scholar-musicians like Professor László Dobszay (Hungary), Dr Mary Berry (England), Marcel Pérès (France) and Professor William Mahrt (USA). Their heroic efforts have inspired a grassroots revival of the Gregorian *schola*, with many new chant choirs springing up in the first years of the twenty-first century, from Orkney to Oregon.

The New Roman Missal

Resources for a revival of sacred music become ever more plentiful. The new *Roman Missal*, published in 2011, includes a simple English setting of the Mass Ordinary based on Gregorian models, and the music for singing almost every part of the Mass is clearly laid out in the Missal itself. The Australian musician Christopher Barlow has produced a volume containing music that will enable ministers and congregations to sing their parts of the Eucharist in both Latin and English. Called simply *Singing the Mass*, it was published by Solesmes in 2011. Good contemporary Mass settings for congregations are getting thicker on the ground. James MacMillan has revised his popular *St Anne's Mass* to conform with the new translation, and several settings have been written specifically for the new texts: one could mention, among others, the same composer's *Mass of Blessed John Henry Newman*, and Jeremy de Satgé's *Missa Melismatica* from the UK; the *Missa Simplex* by Michael O'Connor and the late Richard Proulx, and the *St Ralph Sherwin Mass* by Jeff Ostrowski from the USA; and the *Psallite* Mass by the international Collegeville Composers Group. In several countries, the faithful now have access to excellent hymn books, e.g. *Cecilia* in Sweden; *Éneklő Egyház* ("The Singing Church") in Hungary; the *St Michael Hymnal* and the *Vatican II Hymnal* in the USA. British publishers have yet to produce a hymn book which is so effectively integrated with the authentic texts and music of the liturgy.

At the same time, choral music of the highest quality continues to be composed for the Catholic liturgy. James MacMillan and Roxana Panufnik have written Masses for Westminster Cathedral Choir; Arvo Pärt from Estonia and Poland's Henryk Górecki are world famous composers whose reputations were established by their liturgical music. The English composer Nicholas Wilton, and the American Kevin Allen - among many others - have written some beautiful motets, suitable for small choirs, which deserve to be better known.

The Sung Mass

We praise you, we bless you, we adore you, we glorify you, we give you thanks for your great glory.

(The *Gloria in excelsis*)

In the early centuries, every celebration of the Eucharist was sung. This is still the case in some of the Eastern Rites. It is all too easy to suppose that Low Mass is the norm, and that music is added on special days. Liturgical history and the witness of the Eastern Churches show us that the reverse is true. Music is not the icing on the cake; it is the leaven that makes it rise.

In the first official instruction on sacred music to appear after the Second Vatican Council, it was proposed that the Mass should be sung as often as possible: "For the celebration of the Eucharist with the people, especially on Sundays and feast days, a form of sung Mass is to be preferred as much as possible, even several times on the same day".[25] The *General Instruction of the Roman Missal* (GIRM) - the official manual for the celebration of Mass - states that:

Great importance should be attached to the use of singing in the celebration of the Mass...Although it is not always necessary (e.g., in weekday Masses) to sing all the texts that are in principle meant to be sung, every care should be taken that singing by the ministers and the people not be absent in celebrations that occur on Sundays and on Holydays of Obligation (GIRM 40).

In the sung Mass, the priest, the deacon, the readers, the choir, the musicians, and the congregation at large all have their own parts to play. This alternation of voices has a practical value - it allows each participant to rest his or her voice while the others sing - but, more than that, it allows the assembled Church to manifest itself as a body made up of distinct members, differing from one another but complementary, as in St Paul's vision of the Church (*1 Co* 12).

The Proper of the Mass

What the priest has to sing is musically quite modest, and is largely based on that simple form of plainsong known as cantillation. If one single thing could be done to catalyse an improvement in liturgical music, my suggestion would be this: let celebrants sing the parts of the Mass which belong to them - at the very least, the dialogue which precedes the Preface, the Preface itself, and the doxology at the end of the Eucharistic Prayer. This, more than anything, will encourage the lay faithful to join in the sacred rites with the "fully conscious and active participation" which the Second Vatican Council enjoined (SC 14).

The term "active participation" must, however, be properly understood. It was first used by Pope St Pius X in 1903: "it is imperative in the first place to give heed to the holiness and worthiness of the temple of God", since it is here that the faithful, through "active participation in the sacred mysteries", draw upon "the authentic spirit of Christ".[26] In 1928, Pope Pius XI spelled out the practical implications of this for liturgical music: "In order that the faithful may more actively participate in divine worship, let them be made once more to sing the Gregorian chant... filled with a deep sense of the beauty of the Liturgy, they should sing alternately with the clergy or the choir, as it is prescribed."[27] Active participation, then, is achieved not by limiting liturgical music to songs that everyone joins in with, but by fostering an alternation of voices in a beautiful, holy and worthy liturgy. As Pope John Paul II said: "Active participation does not preclude the active passivity of silence, stillness and listening: indeed it demands it. Worshippers are not passive, for instance, when listening to...the chants and music of the liturgy."[28]

The Ordinary of the Mass

To participate fully in the sung Mass, the laity should make the responses to the acclamations of the priest, deacon, lector and psalmist, and they should sing at least part of the

Mass Ordinary and the Lord's Prayer. The **Ordinary of the Mass** is a set of liturgical songs whose texts are invariable; they can, however, be sung to many different settings. The official Latin chant books contain eighteen numbered sets of *Kyrie*, *Gloria*, *Sanctus* and *Agnus Dei*; there are moreover half a dozen chant settings of the *Credo*. In the new English translation of the *Roman Missal*, there is an English plainsong setting of the Ordinary, which is based on some of the Latin chants. There are also, of course, innumerable choral settings of these texts, and some congregational settings of the new English Ordinary are already available. The Ordinary consists of the following elements:

- The *Kyrie* is one of two chants in the Western liturgy which are in Greek (the other is the *Agios o Theos* of the Good Friday Liturgy). The simple text - "Lord, have mercy. Christ, have mercy." - was probably once the refrain of a litany, imported from the Greek liturgy in the sixth century and left untranslated. The invocations of the litany have been lost, but the response remains. The setting suggested in the new *Roman Missal* is taken from the Ordinary that is listed in official editions of the chant books as Mass XVI; this *Kyrie* melody is first found in manuscripts of the eleventh century. The new Missal gives the text in both Greek and English.

- The **Gloria in excelsis** is one of the earliest Christian liturgical texts, going back possibly to the second century. Like the *Kyrie*, it is Greek in origin, but was translated into Latin when it was adopted into the Roman Mass, perhaps in the fourth century. At first, it was recited only by bishops, and only at Christmas. The opening words are of course those uttered by the angels at the birth of Christ: "Glory to God in the highest, and on earth peace to people of good will" (*Lk* 2:13). Over the centuries, the use of the *Gloria* was extended to all priests, and to other occasions in the Church's year, until eventually it became a congregational chant for every Sunday and feast day, being omitted only in Advent and Lent. The new *Roman Missal* provides an English *Gloria* based on the one in Mass XV. This tenth-century melody, with its simple, repeating pattern of rise and fall, is the oldest and simplest version of the *Gloria*.

- The **Credo** was originally not a liturgical text at all, but a declaration of orthodox belief published by the Council of Constantinople in 381. It was adopted into the baptismal rite, and then (in the sixth century) into the Greek Eucharistic Liturgy. Rome adopted the Creed into the rite of Mass only in 1014. It is sung on Sundays and the most important feast days only. The new Missal offers a choice of English settings:

one based on the ancient *Credo* I; or another based on the much later, but very popular *Credo* III. GIRM also mentions the Creed as one of the chants which all Catholics should be able to sing in Latin.

- The **Sanctus** is the oldest of the Ordinary chants; it is mentioned by St Clement of Rome at the end of the first century. The *Sanctus* weaves together several scriptural allusions: Isaiah 6:3; Revelation 4:8; Psalm 117:26; Matthew 21:9. Like the angels, we praise God for his holiness; like the people of Jerusalem, we praise Christ who comes to us in his Father's name. The simple setting in the Missal is taken from Mass XVIII: it is a thirteenth-century chant.

- The **Agnus Dei** was introduced around 700. Its text is inspired by the testimony of John the Baptist: "Behold the Lamb of God, who takes away the sin of the world" (*Jn* 1:29). It accompanies the breaking of the consecrated Host: the Body of the spotless Lamb. The twelfth-century melody printed in the Missal is drawn from Mass XVIII.

The Liturgy of the Word

When considering the **Liturgy of the Word**, it is worth bearing in mind that this part of the Mass was sung *in its entirety* until within living memory; and this is also the practice in the Eastern Churches. It remains an option in the modern Roman rite. The Old Testament, New Testament and Gospel readings can be chanted by the priest or deacon and lectors using a pattern of slight musical inflections to mark the punctuation of the lessons; tones for chanting the readings are given in the new English edition of the Missal. Even chanting a lesson on a monotone lends a greater solemnity to the proclamation. On the principle that "in the choosing of the parts actually to be sung, preference is to be given to those that are of greater importance" (GIRM 40), it is especially fitting that the Gospel should be chanted, if possible.

The Psalm which follows the first reading was, in the early Church, regarded as a lesson in its own right; but owing to the inherent lyrical qualities of the Psalter, it was always sung in a slightly more expressive manner. The Tract, the most primitive chant in the whole Mass Proper, consists simply of a series - sometimes extremely long - of Psalm verses in an elaborate chant setting, originally sung by a soloist. At Rome, the **Tract** was eventually supplanted (except in Lent) by the **Gradual**, which consists of a refrain (sung by the *schola*) and a Psalm verse (sung by a solo cantor); in modern practice the refrain is not usually repeated. In North Africa and the East, another manner of singing the Psalm developed: in the **Responsorial Psalm**, the verses were sung by a soloist, and the people answered with a simple refrain after each verse.

The **Alleluia** (or **Alleluiatic Verse**) developed somewhat later, around 700; it has the following structure: "Alleluia, alleluia. [Scriptural verse.] Alleluia." This chant is characterised by the long, ecstatic melisma (extended flurry of notes) on the final syllable of "alleluia". It is a vocal fanfare, preparing us for the announcement of good news in the Gospel. During the Easter season, the Gradual is replaced by an Alleluia, so that there are two Alleluiatic Verses at each Mass. From the ninth century, singers sometimes fitted new words to the notes of the melisma on "alleluia", and in time this became an independent chant: the **Sequence**. Rhymed, metrical Sequences proliferated in the later middle ages, but only a few found their way into the Roman Missal of 1570. The current liturgical books contain just four Sequences: *Victimæ Paschali* in Easter Week; *Veni Sancte Spiritus* at Pentecost; *Lauda Sion* for Corpus Christi; and *Stabat Mater* on the feast of Our Lady of Sorrows (15th September). There is no reason why other examples of the best Sequences from the tradition cannot be introduced *ad libitum*, such as the Christmas Sequence *Lætabundus*, or Sequences in honour of local saints.

The structure of the Liturgy of the Word, if sung according to the *Graduale*, varies according to the season:

- *In Lent*. Old Testament reading - Gradual - New Testament reading - Tract - Gospel

- *In Eastertide*. Reading from Acts - Alleluia - NT reading - Alleluia - [Sequence] - Gospel

- *At other times*. OT reading - Gradual - NT reading - Alleluia - [Sequence] - Gospel

In the Lectionary (the book of readings), the Proper chants are not reproduced. Instead, the first reading is followed by a **Responsorial Psalm**. Unfortunately, we know only a few of the texts that were formerly used for this kind of Psalm recitation, and none of the melodies, as the practice died out at an early date. The Responsorial Psalms that we have now are, therefore, modern reconstructions, which were inserted into the Roman Lectionary in 1969. In the Lectionary, the Gospel lesson is immediately preceded by a **Gospel Acclamation**. Normally, this has the same structure as the traditional Alleluia; during Lent, the word "alleluia" is replaced with some other short formula of praise. The Church has published no official musical settings for these texts of the Lectionary, but many settings of the Responsorial Psalms are available, and the Gospel Acclamations can readily be set to the old melismatic Alleluia tones, or to a simpler melody for the whole congregation to sing.

Processional Chants and Hymns

One ought to sing the *Mass*, *and not just sing* during
the Mass.[29]

(Consilium for the Implementation
of the Constitution on the Sacred Liturgy)

Besides the chants mentioned in the previous chapter,
the *Graduale Romanum* also includes the **processional
Proper chants**, which are as follows: the Introit, the
Offertory, and the Communion.

Entrance antiphon

The **Introit** accompanies the procession of the celebrant
and ministers to the altar. This chant seems to have
developed in the early sixth century, possibly in connection
with the "stational Mass" - the Roman custom whereby
the Pope (and his *schola*) processed to different churches
around the city to celebrate Mass on certain days. The
opening words of the best known Introits have given their
names to some of the most important liturgical days and
rites, e.g. *Gaudete* Sunday, the *Requiem* Mass.

The **Offertory** chant accompanies the procession which
brings bread and wine to the altar. In early manuscripts,
a refrain alternates with solo verses, but it later became

customary to omit the verses. As with most of the Proper chants, the text is commonly drawn from the Psalms.

At both of these moments, the rubrics of the Missal permit the replacement of the *Graduale Romanum* chant with an appropriate chant from the *Graduale Simplex*, or "another chant that is suited to the sacred action, the day, or the time of year, and whose text has been approved by the Conference of Bishops" (GIRM 48, 74). In practice, "another chant" frequently takes the form of a congregational hymn in English.

Communion antiphon

In the early centuries, the chant at communion time was invariably Psalm 33, with verse 9 as a refrain: "Taste and see that the Lord is good". Later, other texts were selected for the **Communion** chant, often because of their Eucharistic imagery or their connection with the gospel reading of the day. This chant is sung *during* the distribution of holy communion; *after* communion, "a Psalm or other canticle of praise or a hymn may also be sung by the whole congregation" (GIRM 87-88).

The Propers contain a rich treasury of Scriptural texts which complement and illuminate the readings at Mass. As the oldest collection of musical compositions still in use, the Latin chants of the Proper unite us with the Church throughout the world, and with the countless generations of Catholics who created, cultivated and restored these masterpieces of sung spirituality. They are, in short, holy, beautiful and universal; and there are definite benefits to preserving - or, where necessary, recovering - these processional chants. They are unmeasured, that is to say, they do not have a regular beat but are rhythmically free. Instead of driving forward like the insistent rhythm of a hymn, therefore, they create a space for unhurried meditation, fostering a sense of devout recollection in the listeners. Because each chant consists of an antiphon alternating with Psalm verses, it is possible to fit the music to the action. Thus, the Introit can be brought to an end as soon as the celebrant is ready to recite the opening prayers of the Mass. If the procession is longer than usual, the chant can be prolonged simply by adding another Psalm verse.

Even if the choir is unable to master all the elaborate melodies of the *Graduale Romanum*, there are a growing number of resources that make the traditional Proper texts available in a less demanding form. The *Graduale Simplex* has already been mentioned. Adam Bartlett's book of *Simple English Propers* sets all the Proper texts (in translation) to easy chant melodies. The Introits for Sundays and feasts have been translated into English metre in Christoph Tietze's *Introit Hymns for the Church Year*, so that a version of the traditional text can be sung by the whole congregation, using familiar hymn tunes.

Congregational hymns

Must we, then, dispense with our hymn books altogether? Surely not: the rich diversity of liturgical music would be impoverished by the complete exclusion of hymns. It is quite possible to integrate a judicious use of hymns with the Proper chants. For example, if the processions of the Mass make use of the full length of a large church, and if incense is used at the entrance and the preparation of the gifts, then there is often time to sing a hymn before intoning the Introit, or to follow the Offertory chant with a hymn. The rubrics specifically provide for a congregational hymn after the Communion chant. At the end of Mass, a recessional hymn is always a possibility.

There is, after all, nothing new about Catholics praising God with hymns. Hymn-singing in the Latin Church took its greatest impetus from St Ambrose of Milan in the fourth century. When St Benedict wrote his Rule for monks in the sixth century, he stipulated that *ambrosiani* - hymns in the style of Ambrose, perhaps, rather than specifically those written by Ambrose himself - should be sung at each hour of prayer during the day. At Rome itself, hymns were admitted into the Divine Office only in the twelfth century. The early Latin Office hymns are generally characterised by their sobriety, their objectivity, and their sophisticated use of imagery drawn from sacred Scripture. The later medieval Sequences at Mass sometimes display more inventive literary forms and a more expressive emotional register. Alongside these Latin hymns for the Mass and Office, the middle ages produced a luxuriance of popular religious songs in local languages: Italian *laude spirituali*, English carols, *cantigas* from Spain and Portugal.

The Protestant tradition

The singing of vernacular, congregational hymns at Mass originated in Germany before the Reformation, but it was the Protestant Martin Luther - himself a skilled musician - who first made vernacular hymns an integral part of an official liturgy. Some of the first Lutheran hymns were intended for the celebration of the communion service, specifically to replace the traditional plainsong of the Latin Mass. By contrast, those Protestants who followed John Calvin rejected hymns, along with all traditional sacred music, and would sing nothing but metrical versions of the Psalms. Among British Protestants, the scrupulous abstinence from hymnody started to break down in the late seventeenth century. The eighteenth century saw the great flowering of English Protestant hymn-writing, with the work of Isaac Watts ("When I survey the wondrous Cross"), Charles Wesley ("Love Divine, all loves excelling") and John Newton ("Amazing Grace"). Traditionalists in the Church of England fought a long rearguard action against the introduction of hymns into the church service itself, but by about 1860 this resistance had crumbled, and the Anglican contribution to English hymnody in the Victorian period is rightly celebrated. Catholics continued to write and sing hymns, but outside the regions of German influence, hymns were associated with popular devotions, processions, parish missions and guild meetings, rather than with the official liturgy of the Church.

For Germany and Austria, where the singing of vernacular hymns at Mass had become a well-established custom, the Holy See gave explicit permission for hymns to *supplement* (1943) and later to *replace* (1967) the processional chants. This permission was extended to the universal Church in 1969, with the promulgation of the new Order of Mass by Pope Paul VI. The results of this concession were a sometimes incautious adoption of hymns from Protestant traditions, some of which should have undergone considerable alteration on doctrinal grounds, and an unprecedented explosion of Catholic liturgical hymn-writing in English.

Catholic hymn books

Open up a typical Catholic hymn book, and you will find hymns reflecting every phase of this long and complex history: early Latin Office hymns in translation; popular Christmas carols; Protestant hymns; Catholic devotional songs in honour of our Lady or the Blessed Sacrament; and hymns of more recent vintage.

Vernacular hymns have many laudable qualities. As songs that involve the whole assembly, they foster unity of mind and heart. As expressions of local and national culture, they adapt worship to the native genius of a particular people. Provided, of course, that they are orthodox, they constitute a sort of sung catechism, conveying Christian truth in an attractive and memorable way. Pope Pius XII declared: "Popular religious hymns are of great help to the Catholic apostolate and should be carefully cultivated and promoted."[30] He also laid down the qualities which hymns ought to have:

- "they must be in full conformity with the doctrine of the Catholic faith";
- "they must also express and explain that doctrine accurately";
- "they must use plain language…and must be free from violent and vain excess of words";
- they must use "simple melody";
- "they should manifest a religious dignity and seriousness";
- and, if used at Mass, it is helpful if they are "properly adapted to the individual parts of the Mass".[31]

Turning the Pope's list on its head, one can identify the characteristics of *bad* hymns: they are doctrinally incorrect, or at least imprecise; they are extravagant and pretentious, or banal and trite; they are at odds with their liturgical context (e.g. referring to the consecrated elements as "bread and wine" in a communion hymn). Hymns have their place at Mass, but they must be of good quality; they must be performed well (even congregational hymns benefit from the support of a good choir or organ accompaniment); and they must not entirely drive out the Proper chants of the liturgy.

Concluding Thoughts

In their mindlessness they involuntarily falsified music itself when they asserted that there was no such thing as correct music, and that it was quite correct to judge music by the standard of the pleasure it gives to whoever enjoys it.

(Plato)

Discussions about liturgical music often focus on questions of aesthetic taste; but this is not the point at issue. Remember Plato's complaint about the poets. If music were merely a decorative addition to the liturgy, then it could indeed be judged good or bad by the pleasure it gave. Liturgical musicians would need to sing and play only what pleased or entertained the congregation. Such is not our Church's way.' "Certainly," as the Holy Father has stated, "as far as the liturgy is concerned, we cannot say that one song is as good as another."[32] On the one hand, the Church does not minutely or prescriptively regulate all that we sing at Mass; on the other hand, liturgical music is not a free-for-all. A small core repertoire of Gregorian chant in Latin is proposed to all the faithful, with particular emphasis on the simple responses (e.g. *Et cum spiritu tuo*), *Credo* III and the *Pater noster*, so that all Catholics can participate together in Masses at international gatherings. At the other end of the scale, certain abuses in church music - a theatrical style, the use of undignified instruments, alterations to the words of the Mass Ordinary - are prohibited.

These minimal precepts leave open a wide range of possible options when decisions about liturgical music are being made. In many cases, it falls to bishops' conferences, individual bishops, pastors or musicians to make decisions about what music should or should not be used in the celebration of the Eucharist. The basic criteria laid down by Pope Pius X - holiness, beauty and universality - remain valid; Gregorian chant and Renaissance polyphony are still held up as permanent touchstones for liturgical music. The Church's criteria for evaluating music in the liturgy were recently summarised by Pope Benedict XVI:

> the sense of prayer, of dignity and of beauty; full adherence to the texts and to the actions of the liturgy; the involvement of the assembly, hence a legitimate adaptation to the local culture while preserving at the same time the universality of the language; the primacy of Gregorian chant as a supreme model of sacred music and the wise use of other modes of expression that are part of the Church's historical and liturgical patrimony, especially, but not only, polyphony; the importance of the *schola cantorum*, particularly in cathedral churches. Today too these are important criteria which should be taken into careful consideration.[33]

If these criteria are applied rigorously, we may discover that some of the music heard in our parishes is not adequate to its sublime purpose. This is a matter that the Church takes very seriously. A recent Vatican instruction states that "it is the *right* of the community of Christ's faithful that especially in the Sunday celebration there should customarily be true and suitable sacred music".[34] Blessed John Paul II called for an examination of conscience on the state of liturgical music. The purpose of such a re-evaluation should not be to denigrate the hard work that countless devoted Catholics have put into music for the liturgy in past decades; but it should inspire us to embrace "true and suitable sacred music".

Suggested Reading

For the Church's recent teaching and legislation on music, see:

- Second Vatican Council, *Sacrosanctum Concilium* (1963), paragraphs 112-121;
- Sacred Congregation for Rites, *Musicam Sacram* (1967);
- *Catechism of the Catholic Church* (1994), 1156-58;
- Pope John Paul II, Chirograph on Sacred Music (2003);
- Pope Benedict XVI, *Sacramentum Caritatis* (2007), 42;
- *General Instruction of the Roman Missal* (new ed., 2011), 39-41, 102-04, 366-67, 393.

Important chapters on the theology of liturgical music are found in *Feast of Faith* (San Francisco, Ignatius, 1986) and *The Spirit of the Liturgy* (San Francisco: Ignatius, 2000) by Joseph Ratzinger, and in *Lost in Wonder* by Aidan Nichols (Farnham, Ashgate, 2011).

The history of Catholic church music is concisely narrated in Edward Schaefer's *Catholic Music through the Ages* (Chicago, Hillenbrand, 2008). *Sacred Music and Liturgical Reform: Treasures and Transformations* (Chicago, Hillenbrand, 2007) by Anthony Ruff provides a more detailed account. *Gregorian Chant* by David Hiley (Cambridge University Press, 2009) is the best introductory guide to the history and theory of chant.

The books of English Propers mentioned on p, 63 are: Adam Bartlett, *Simple English Propers* (Richmond, CMAA, 2011); and Christoph Tietze, *Introit Hymns for the Church Year* (Franklin Park, World Library Publications, 2005). The standard work on hymns in English is J.R. Watson's *The English Hymn* (Oxford University Press, 1997). Ian Bradley's *'Daily Telegraph' Book of Hymns* (London, Continuum, 2006) gives commentaries on 150 popular hymns. The present author is preparing an annotated anthology of Catholic hymns.

Three books by US musicians deserve careful study by anyone involved in Catholic church music today: *Why Catholics Can't Sing* by Thomas Day (New York, Crossroad, 1995); *The Musical Shape of the Liturgy* by William Mahrt (Richmond, CMAA, 2012); and *Sacred Treasure: Understanding Catholic Liturgical Music* by Joseph P. Swain (Collegeville, Pueblo, 2012).

Useful websites to visit include the following:

- The Gregorian Chant Network
  (*www.gregorianchantnetwork.org*);
- The Blessed John Henry Newman Institute of Liturgical Music
  (*www.oratorymusic.org.uk*);
- The Church Music Association of America (*musicasacra.com*);
- Music for the Liturgy
  (*www.ccwatershed.org/liturgy*);
- The Chant Café blog (*www.chantcafe.com*);
- The Liturgy Office of the Catholic Bishops' Conference of
  England & Wales (*www.liturgyoffice.org.uk/Resources/Music/
  index.shtml*);
- Roman Missal Scotland (*romanmissalscotland.org.uk/music-
  resources.html*);
- The Society of St Gregory (*www.ssg.org.uk*).

Suggested Listening

There are innumerable recordings of sacred music, and they continue to
proliferate. The following list of CDs is a personal selection.

Learning aids for singing the Mass:

And with your Spirit, Jeremy de Satgé and Patrizia Kwella (The
Music Makers) [the music of the new English Missal]

Orate Fratres, Schola Cantamus/directed by Jeremy de Satgé (The
Music Makers) [Latin chant for priests and deacons]

Chant:

Chant of the Early Christians, Ensemble Organum/Marcel Pérès
(Harmonia Mundi)

Christmas in Royal Anglo-Saxon Winchester, Schola Gregoriana of
Cambridge/Mary Berry (Herald AV)

Voices: Chant from Avignon, The Benedictine Nuns of Notre-Dame
de l'Annonciation (Decca)

Medieval:

Hildegard, *A Feather on the Breath of God*, Gothic Voices/Christopher Page (Hyperion)

A Scottish Lady Mass: Sacred Music from Medieval St Andrews, Red Byrd (Hyperion)

Dunstable, *Sweet Harmony: Masses and Motets*, Tonus Peregrinus/ Antony Pitts (Naxos)

Renaissance:

Palestrina, *Masses*, Pro Cantione Antiqua/Bruno Turner (Brilliant Classics)

Victoria, *Requiem*, Gabrieli Consort/Paul McCreesh (Archiv)

Byrd, *The Three Masses*, Tallis Scholars/Peter Phillips (Gimell)

Baroque:

Monteverdi, *Vespers of the Blessed Virgin*, Monteverdi Choir/John Eliot Gardiner (Archiv)

La Messe du Roi: Music from the Court of the Sun King, Ensemble Dumont/Peter Bennett (Linn)

Classical:

Mozart, *Coronation Mass*, Academy of Ancient Music/Christopher Hogwood (Decca)

Haydn, *The Complete Mass Edition*, Collegium Musicum 90/Richard Hickox (Chaconne)

Modern:

Fauré, *Requiem - Messe Basse*, Westminster Cathedral Choir/David Hill (Alto)

Duruflé, *Requiem - Mass 'Cum Jubilo'*, Westminster Cathedral Choir/ James O'Donnell (Hyperion)

Contemporary:

James MacMillan, *Who are these Angels?* New Choral Music, Cappella Nova/Alan Tavener (Lynn)

Nicholas Wilton, *Sacred Choral Music*, Magnificat/Philip Cave (Philangelus)

Endnotes

[1] John Paul II, General Audience (26th February 2003).

[2] Joseph Ratzinger, *The Feast of Faith* (San Francisco, Ignatius Press, 1986), p. 122.

[3] Benedict XVI, Letter to the Bishops on the Publication of the Apostolic Letter *Summorum Pontificum* (7th July 2007).

[4] Augustine of Hippo, *Sermon 336*.1 (PL 38.1472); my translation.

[5] Ratzinger, *The Feast of Faith*, p. 101.

[6] Second Vatican Council, Constitution on the Sacred Liturgy, *Sacrosanctum Concilium* (4th December 1963), paragraph 112.

[7] Pliny, Letter 10.96, in Pliny the Younger, *Complete Letters*, translated by P.G. Walsh (Oxford, Oxford University Press, 2006), pp. 278-79.

[8] *The Rule of Saint Benedict* 19, translated by Justin McCann (London, Sheed and Ward, 1976), pp. 31-32.

[9] Ratzinger, *The Feast of Faith*, p. 100.

[10] Plato, *Timaeus* 47c-d, translated by H.D.P. Lee (London, Penguin, 1977), p. 65.

[11] Plato, *Laws* 700e, translated by Thomas L. Pangle (Chicago, University of Chicago Press, 1988), p. 86.

[12] Clement of Rome, *Letter to the Corinthians* 34, in *Early Christian Writings*, translated by Maxwell Staniforth (Harmondsworth, Penguin, 1968), pp. 40-41.

[13] Ignatius of Antioch, *Letter to the Ephesians* 4, in *Early Christian Writings*, p. 76.

[14] Augustine of Hippo, *Confessions* 10.33.50 (PL 32.800); my translation.

[15] Augustine, *Confessions* 9.6.14 (PL 32.769-70).

[16] Augustine, *Confessions* 10.33.50 (PL 32.800).

[17] Hildegard of Bingen, *Letter to the Prelates of Mainz* (PL 197.220-21); my translation.

[18] Hildegard, *Letter to the Prelates of Mainz*, (PL 197.200).

[19] Thomas Aquinas, *Summa Theologica* (2.2 Q.91 a.2), quoted in Ratzinger, *The Feast of Faith*, p. 121.

[20] Ratzinger, *The Feast of Faith*, p. 100.

[21] Ratzinger, *The Feast of Faith*, p. 125.

[22] Robert Richardson, *Commentary on the Rule of St Augustine* (Edinburgh, Scottish History Society, 1935), pp. 80-81; my translation.

[23] Sacred Congregation for Divine Worship, Letter to the Bishops on the Minimum Repertoire of Plainchant, *Voluntati Obsequens* (14th April 1974).

[24] Benedict XVI, Greeting during the Blessing of the New Organ, Alte Kapelle, Regensburg (13th September 2006).

[25] Sacred Congregation of Rites, Instruction on Music in the Liturgy, *Musicam Sacram* (5th March 1967), 27.

[26] Pius X, Motu Proprio, *Tra le sollecitudini* (22nd November 1903).

[27] Pius XI, Apostolic Constitution, *Divini cultus sanctitatem* (20th December 1928).

[28] John Paul II, Address to Bishops from the US (9th October 1998).

[29] Consilium for the Implementation of the Constitution on the Sacred Liturgy, Notification, *Cantare la Messa* (1969).

[30] Pius XII, Encyclical, *Musicae Sacrae* (25th December 1955), 37.

[31] Pius XII, *Musicae Sacrae* 63-64.

[32] Benedict XVI, Apostolic Exhortation, *Sacramentum Caritatis* (22nd February 2007), 42.

[33] Benedict XVI, Letter on the Centenary of the Foundation of the Pontifical Institute of Sacred Music (13th May 2011).

[34] Congregation for Divine Worship and the Discipline of the Sacraments, Instruction, *Redemptionis sacramentum* (25th March 2004), 57 (emphasis added).

Participating in the Mass

Dom Cuthbert Johnson OSB

A guide to active prayerful participation in the holy sacrifice of the Mass.

Abbot Cuthbert Johnson OSB, in this companion to his widely acclaimed CTS booklet Understanding the Roman Missal, provides an informative, step-by-step guide to the celebration of the Mass, to enable the Liturgy to be celebrated with reverence, dignity and beauty.

Abbot Cuthbert writes: "Every member of the worshipping community present at Mass has the responsibility of participating in the Liturgy in such a way as to contribute to the splendour of Divine Worship for the glory and praise of God."

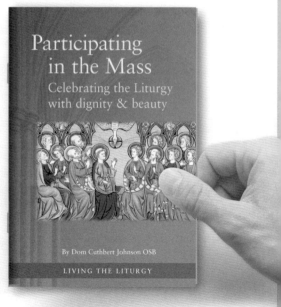

LT 03   ISBN 978 1 86082 758 7

A world of Catholic reading at your fingertips...

Catholic Faith, Life & Truth for all

www.cts-online.org.uk

ctscatholiccompass.org

twitter: @CTSpublishers

facebook.com/CTSpublishers

Catholic Truth Society, Publishers to the Holy See.

The Order of Mass
with Music Cards

With New English Translation

Set on durable laminated card, this participation aid features the text of the new English translation of the Order of Mass, plus the new official musical settings created for it.

It is elegantly set out in red and black, with musical annotation in a new, simplified style - an easy to follow, helpful guide for all participants in the Mass.

CTS Code: PC76-P